MEET THE GREATS

SACAGAWEA

TIM COOKE

Gareth Stevens
PUBLISHING

Please visit our website, **www.garethstevens.com**.
For a free color catalog of all our high-quality books,
call toll free 1-800-542-2595 or fax 1-877-542-2596.

CATALOGING-IN-PUBLICATION DATA

Names: Cooke, Tim.
Title: Sacagawea / Tim Cooke.
Description: New York : Gareth Stevens, 2017. | Series: Meet the greats | Includes index.
Identifiers: ISBN 9781482459609 (pbk.) | ISBN 9781482459623 (library bound) | ISBN 9781482459616 (6 pack)
Subjects: LCSH: Sacagawea--Juvenile literature. | Lewis and Clark Expedition (1804-1806)--Juvenile literature. | Shoshoni women--Biography--Juvenile literature.
Classification: LCC F592.7.S123 C66 2017 | DDC 978.0049745740092--dc23

Published in 2017 by
Gareth Stevens Publishing
111 East 14th Street, Suite 349
New York, NY 10003

For Brown Bear Books Ltd:
Editorial Director: Lindsey Lowe
Managing Editor: Tim Cooke
Children's Publisher: Anne O'Daly
Design Manager: Keith Davis
Designer and illustrator: Supriya Sahai
Picture Manager: Sophie Mortimer

Concept development: Square and Circus / Brown Bear Books Ltd

Picture Credits: Front Cover: Character artwork, Supriya Sahai. Interior: 123rf: Steve Estvanik 23; American Philosophical Society: 42b; Dreamstime: Bryant Aardema 40, Tom Dowd 10b, Charles Knowles 39, Dave Macleavy 41, Spela Znidarsic 8t; istockphoto: 9; Library of Congress: 14, 18t, 21t, 21b, 31, 32, 33, 42t, State Historical Society of North Dakota 21t; Shutterstock: 15, Thomas Brain 25b, Cynoclub 26, Everett Historical 28, 25t, 35br, Martidis Ioannis 29, Gail Johnson 24, Frank L. Junior 34, Leigh Anne Meeks 11, netfall 43t, Denton Rumsey 13; Wikipedia: Boston Museum of Fine Arts 25t, Denver Art Museum/Google Cultural Institute 10t, EncMstr 43b, Gooseterrain 19, 22, Matt Lavin 38, Montana State Capitol/Edgar Samuel Paxson 30, US Department of Defence 18b, Walters Art Museum/commissioned by William T. L. Walters, 1858-1860 12, 20t, 20b.

Printed in the United States of America
CPSIA compliance information: Batch CW17GS: For further information contact Gareth Stevens, New York, New York at 1-800-542-2595.

Contents

Introduction 4

A Shoshone Upbringing 6

Feature: Native American Navigation 14

Captivity and Marriage 16

Feature: The Fur Trappers 24

Guiding Lewis and Clark 26

Feature: Sacagawea's Baby 34

Back from the Pacific 36

Timeline 44

Glossary 46

Further Resources 47

Index 48

Introduction

Sacagawea played a key role in the creation of the modern United States when she helped guide explorers across the West.

In 1803, President Thomas Jefferson doubled the size of the United States when he bought what was then called Louisiana from France. In 1804, Jefferson sent his secretary, Meriwether Lewis (1774–1809), and a soldier, William Clark (1770–1838), to explore the vast new territory.

Lewis and Clark headed west up the Missouri River. They hoped the river might lead all the way to the Pacific Ocean. Neither man spoke any Native American languages, so they knew they would need **interpreters** and guides. Near the start of the journey they met Sacagawea, who was from the Lemhi Shoshone tribe. Sacagawea was married to a **fur trapper**, Toussaint Charbonneau, when Lewis and Clark hired her as a guide and interpreter. Her knowledge of landmarks, local **flora** and **fauna**, and different Native American peoples helped make the expedition a success.

A Shoshone UPBRINGING

As a child, Sacagawea learned the traditional ways of life followed by generations of Lemhi Shoshone.

Almost nothing is known about Sacagawea's early life. She was born into the Lemhi Shoshone, who are sometimes called the Northern Shoshone. The tribe lived in the mountainous lands of what is now Idaho. The Shoshone did not keep written records, so we are not sure when Sacagawea was actually born. Many experts estimate that she was born in 1788, although it might have been a year before or after. It was a key time in American history. In 1789 George Washington was sworn in as the first president of the newly independent United States.

QUICK FACTS

- Sacagawea's Shoshone people ate roots and berries, salmon, and buffalo meat.
- She learned where to find food from her mother!

Sacagawea was brought up on the edge of the Rocky Mountains.

Sacagawea was born in the West, probably near the border of the present-day states of Idaho and Montana near the **Continental Divide**. The region was so far from the areas of European settlement that no white people had ever been there. The young girl grew up on the Salmon River in Idaho, surrounded by the Rocky Mountains.

A SHOSHONE CHILDHOOD

Some accounts of Sacagawea's early life say that her original Shoshone name was Boinaiv, which means "Grass Woman." The reason for the name is not known, but Native American names were sometimes based on a talent or an interest.

Sacagawea was given the name by which she is best known later, after she had been kidnapped by the Hidatsa tribe. Sacagawea means "Bird Woman." Perhaps she was first named Grass Woman because grass was vital to the Shoshone people. It was eaten by the animals they hunted, such as the buffalo. Buffalo provided meat, and skins to make clothes. Sacagawea's mother taught her daughter how to find food when there was no meat or fish. Sacagawea learned where to find berries and edible roots, and to identify which were poisonous. Later, this knowledge would be vital to the Lewis and Clark expedition.

The Shoshone and other native peoples hunted buffalo on the plains.

This **romantic** painting shows a Shoshone camp by a river.

THE LEMHI SHOSHONE

The homelands of the Lemhi Shoshone were in what is now northern Utah and Idaho. In the spring and summer, they lived on the Idaho side of the territory near the Lemhi and Salmon Rivers, where they caught salmon. Sacagawea's mother taught her daughter how to preserve the fish so they could eat it year-round. In the fall, the salmon swam upstream to **spawn**. That marked the end of the fishing season.

Sockeye salmon turn red as they prepare to spawn.

The **headwaters** of the Missouri River flow through the Three Forks region.

Once fall set in, the Shoshone moved east across the Bitterroot Mountains in search of food. They spent winter in the Three Forks area of the Missouri River. From there, they could hunt the buffalo on the plains.

SKILLED WITH HORSES

The Shoshone were known as skilled horse riders. Horses had first been introduced to the American continent by Spanish explorers in Mexico in 1519. Wild horses had spread north. Historians think the Shoshone may have used horses as early as 1680. They rode in small groups to hunt buffalo or to fight rival native peoples, who competed with them for buffalo or raided them to steal horses.

The Shoshone stretched buffalo hides over wooden poles to make conical tents.

USEFUL SKILLS

The Shoshone originally lived in grass huts, but later they learned from native peoples on the plains to make **tepees** from buffalo skins. When Sacagawea was growing up, she lived in a tepee. She knew how to skin a buffalo, and she helped her mother find food and make clothes and blankets from the buffalo skins. Sometimes, she ate buffalo meat raw because she was too hungry to wait until it had been cooked!

LIVING WITH NATURE

Like other native peoples, the Lemhi Shoshone knew the landscape well. They could tell when the weather was about to change by observing the sky and the wind. They knew how to sense danger such as wildfires from watching the behavior of animals. The Shoshone also knew how to find water, and the best places to cross mountain ranges or set up camp.

A HUSBAND

For the Shoshone, children were vital to the survival of the tribe. When Sacawagea was still young, her parents picked out a young man they thought would be a good husband for her. We do not know if Sacagawea and the man were friends. However, before the two could be married and have children, something happened that changed Sacagawea's life forever.

The Bitterroot Mountains had a harsh winter climate.

Native American NAVIGATION

Sacagawea was able to act as a guide to the Lewis and Clark expedition because she was familiar with Shoshone methods of navigation.

The Shoshone headed east every year before the first snow of winter arrived and they knew the best route to take. They made their own maps, but they were not like the type of maps Lewis and Clark drew of their expedition. Shoshone and other native peoples drew maps on animal skins or sheets of bark from birch trees. Sometimes, they were drawn in sand to plan a route before setting out on a journey.

Native American maps did not show **scale** as western maps did. Instead, they often indicated how long it took to travel to a place.

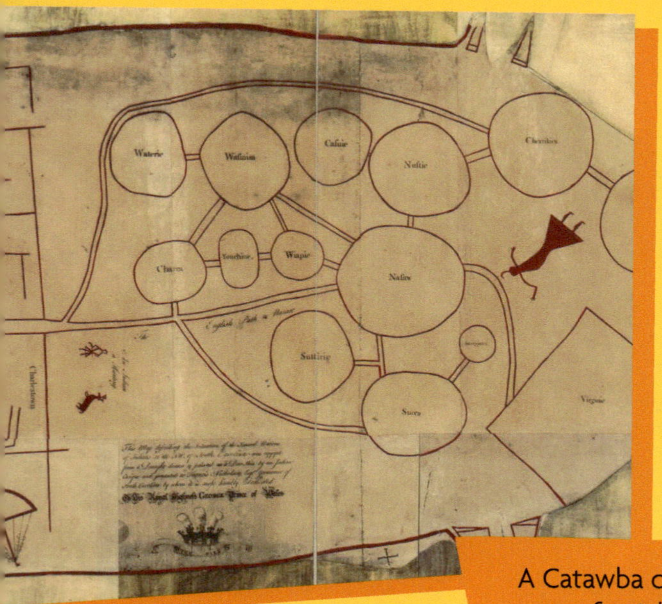

A Catawba chief in South Carolina drew this map of neighboring native peoples in 1721. The English names were added later.

The Big Dipper (also known as the Plow) shows the location of the North Star, at top left.

Maps also marked landmarks, such as a pile of boulders or a rock formation. Lines drawn between places on the maps might show rivers, game trails, or warpaths. Maps were not always **oriented** the same way. The top of the map often pointed toward the sunrise or sunset.

LOOKING AT THE STARS

Native Americans also used the location of the stars and **constellations** to help them navigate and keep track of the seasons. Every year, for example, when the two stars they called the "swimming ducks" appeared in the night sky in the West, it meant it was almost time to plant their crops.

Captivity and MARRIAGE

Sacagawea's life with the Shoshone ended suddenly when she was kidnapped at the age of about 12 years old.

In 1800, Sacagawea was traveling east through the mountains near her home with a Shoshone hunting party. Suddenly, a group of Hidatsa attacked. The Hidatsa tribe had guns but the Shoshone did not. Sacagawea tried to escape the attackers by diving into a river, but one of the Hidatsa jumped into the water after her and captured her. Other young Shoshone girls were seized at the same time. It was common for native peoples to raid other tribes and take their horses, and take people as slaves. The Hidatsa may have wanted to capture young women as wives for their young men.

QUICK FACTS

- The Hidatsa gave Sacagawea her name, which means "bird woman."
- She may have gotten married when her husband won her in a bet.

Hidatsa warriors celebrated their victories over other native tribes with dances.

HIDATSA LIFE

The Hidatsa were **hunter-gatherers**, like the Shoshone, but they were also farmers. They lived on the plains and grew crops such as corn, beans, and squash. Sacagawea was taken to a Hidatsa village in what is now Bismarck, North Dakota. The Hidatsa shared the village with another tribe, the Mandan. Sacagawea worked for a Hidatsa family. She was used to hard work, but here she no longer had her family for companionship—just the other Shoshone captives.

The Mandan lived in dome-shaped earth huts.

Hidatsa women were responsible for growing crops, while the men hunted buffalo. Women also had to build the domed grass **lodges** in which the Hidatsa lived. They built a framework from poles and then covered it with grass mats and earth to keep it warm. It was the women's job to keep the lodge tidy and clean, cook the food, and take care of the children. Life was busy.

A FUR TRAPPER

Sacagawea had only lived with the Hidatsa for a number of months, although no one is sure exactly how long, before her life changed again. When she was 13 or 14 years old, the Hidatsa decided to sell her to a fur trapper named Toussaint Charbonneau. Charbonneau was a French Canadian who hunted beaver and other animals in the **wilderness**. He also traded with Native American tribes to buy the furs they hunted. Like other trappers, Charbonneau often lived with native peoples.

Women helped keep the inside of lodges clean.

Fur trappers lived for months in the wilderness.

MARRIAGE

Charbonneau and Sacagawea were married. He was at least 20 years older than she was. Charbonneau had already married another Native American woman, but it was usual at the time for a European man to marry more than one native wife. Some experts claim that Charbonneau won Sacagawea in a bet, but it is more likely that the marriage was part of a trade deal. Sacagawea was at an age when it would have been normal for her elders to arrange a match for her. Charbonneau would have given her Hidatsa family valuable goods such as horses in exchange for allowing her to become his wife.

It was quite common for fur trappers to marry native women.

There were about 130 lodges in the Hidatsa-Mandan village.

After their marriage, Sacagawea and Charbonneau continued to live in the Hidatsa-Mandan village. Life continued for Sacagawea as before, only now she was cooking for her husband and making his clothes. Charbonneau was familiar with Hidatsa life, and they lived peacefully with the tribe.

Lewis and Clark spent the winter of 1804 to 1805 with the Hidatsa.

NEW ARRIVALS

In November 1804, Meriwether Lewis and William Clark arrived in the area. By then, Sacagawea was six months pregnant with her first child.

Like the original, this reconstruction of Fort Mandan is built from local cottonwood.

LEWIS AND CLARK

Lewis and Clark and more than 30 soldiers, whom they called the Corps of Discovery, had traveled along the Missouri River. Soon snow and ice would make travel impossible. The explorers decided to spend the winter in the area. They built Fort Mandan and settled in for a long stay.

One of Lewis's and Clark's jobs in the winter of 1804 was to find an interpreter. They would need to buy horses later in their journey. They met Charbonneau and explained what they would need to travel west and on to the Pacific Ocean. Charbonneau was eager to join the expedition, and offered his services.

Lewis and Clark were not sure about hiring Charbonneau. They thought he might be too old. Also, he could not speak Shoshone. Sacagawea had accompanied her husband to the meeting, however, and had given Lewis and Clark buffalo skins to keep them warm. They liked her immediately. They asked Charbonneau if his wife was a Shoshone. When he confirmed that she was a Shoshone and that her people had horses, Lewis and Clark decided to hire the fur trapper—but only if he brought Sacagawea along with him.

A NEW BABY

On February 11, 1805, Sacagawea gave birth to a baby boy. His father called him Jean-Baptiste, but Sacagawea called him "Pomp," which in Shoshone means "firstborn." The new baby would be going on the expedition as well!

This statue of Lewis and Clark was erected in 1990 at the end point of their journey in Oregon.

The FUR TRAPPERS

Toussaint Charbonneau was just one of many fur trappers in the West. Fur was in demand in Europe, so the trade was very profitable.

Fur had become a valuable trading **commodity** in Europe during the 1700s. It was popular for making fashionable coats and hats. Not only did fur keep people warm at a time when most houses were poorly heated, fur was also a **status symbol**, so people paid high prices for the finest furs. The most desirable was beaver fur. Trappers in North America also hunted otter, mink, and fox to send to Europe.

The Dutch and French dominated the early fur trade. In New France—a French **colony** in what is now Canada—the economy was dominated by fur. The city of Quebec had been founded in 1608 as a fur trading post.

Millions of beaver lived along North America's rivers.

Some trappers took their families with them into the West.

Trapping animals was hard, lonely, and often dangerous work. By the 1700s, fur trappers were trading directly with native peoples, swapping items such as knives, metal pots, mirrors, beads, guns, and ammunition in return for furs. Traders could make huge profits: a beaver **pelt** could be bought in North America for one ax head. In Europe, the pelt was worth the equivalent of 12 ax heads. Charbonneau worked as a trapper for the two largest fur companies: the North West Company and the Hudson's Bay Company.

A beaver-skin hat.

Guiding Lewis AND CLARK

While the trip westward took Lewis and Clark into new territory, for Sacagawea it was a return to the land of her childhood.

At the start of April 1805, just seven weeks after Sacagawea had given birth to little Pomp, the Corps of Discovery was ready to begin the next stage of its journey. The expedition would leave Fort Mandan and use canoes to head up the Missouri River. Eventually, Lewis and Clark hoped to find a usable water route to the Pacific Ocean. Such a route would allow the United States to trade with Asia.

The party that set out up the river included 31 men, Sacagawea, her new baby, and Lewis's black Newfoundland dog, Seaman.

Lewis's dog, Seaman, made the whole trip to the Pacific. He would have looked like this dog.

QUICK FACTS

- Thomas Jefferson thought Lewis and Clark might find woolly mammoths in the West.
- The trip led Sacagawea back to her Shoshone homeland!

TAKING THE BABY

Pomp the baby was already popular with the members of the expedition. Captain Clark had given Sacagawea a belt of blue beads to mark the baby's birth. Both Clark and Lewis had studied a little about medicine before starting their journey, because they knew there would be no doctors where they were going. They checked that Sacagawea and Pomp were healthy enough to set off. Sacagawea strapped Pomp to her back in a **papoose**. That was how he traveled all the way to the Pacific Ocean.

Pomp traveled on Sacagawea's back in a papoose.

MAKING GOOD PROGRESS

The Corps of Discovery had eight large canoes. The men rowed upstream against the current. When the wind was in the right direction, they put up sails. They made good progress during April 1805, averaging around 15 miles (24 km) a day. They stopped each night to set up camp.

While the men made the camp, Sacagawea walked along the riverbank, prodding the ground with a pointed stick. She was looking for wild artichokes, which mice sometimes buried. Her mother had taught Sacagawea how to find them. She also found and cooked other roots. They were all unknown to Lewis and Clark, but the men were grateful to try them. Their **staple** diet was meat and bread, which was very boring. Any kind of berries or root vegetables were a welcome change.

Sacagawea found artichoke roots mice had buried to eat in the winter.

Sacagawea helped guide the expedition.

TRACKING SKILLS

As the weeks passed, Sacagawea proved valuable to the Corps of Discovery in a range of ways. One night when they camped, the expedition found the remains of a Native American fire. There were also many tracks nearby.

The explorers were nervous that they might be in the territory of a hostile tribe. Sacagawea examined the tracks. From the marks left by their **moccasins**, she could tell that the tracks did not belong to the feet of a war party. They must have been left by a peaceful group.

NEAR DISASTER!

By mid May, snowmelt was flowing into the Missouri River. It was hard for the boats to sail upstream. One day, the wind rose, forming huge waves. Sacagawea and Pomp were in a boat with all of Lewis and Clark's records of their journey. As a gust of wind caught the sail, Charbonneau steered the wrong way, causing water to flood into the canoe. He panicked because he could not swim. Sacagawea took over. She stopped the records and other supplies from floating away while one of the other men righted the boat. Thanks to her, everything was recovered.

The expedition suffered from a number of **capsizes**.

SACAGAWEA FALLS SICK

The journey continued to be tough. Early in June, Sacagawea became so sick with a high fever that Captain Clark feared she would die. It took her a week to recover. A few days later, the party were in a deep canyon when a hailstorm began. They sheltered under an overhanging rock, when suddenly a flash flood rushed through the canyon. Sacagawea saved Pomp just before his papoose was swept away. Then Clark pushed Sacagawea and her baby up the steep hillside as the water rushed past.

THE SHOSHONE CHIEF

On August 8, Sacagawea recognized the shape of a hill she had known as a small child. She knew the expedition was getting close to her homeland.

Sacagawea recognized the headwaters of the Missouri River.

The explorers met more than 30 different Native American peoples.

On August 17, 1805, Lewis and Clark met a group of Shoshone. They invited the Shoshone chief to their camp. They hoped to persuade him to sell them horses, and needed Sacagawea to act as their interpreter.

When Sacagawea met the chief she could not believe her eyes. It was her brother, Cameahwait! They had not seen each other since her kidnapping. Sacagawea told her brother that the explorers came in peace. Cameahwait was happy to sell them horses for the dangerous trip across the Rocky Mountains. But Sacagawea now had a difficult choice to make. Should she stay with her people, or travel on and see the Pacific Ocean?

Sacagawea's BABY

Jean-Baptiste Charbonneau (1805–1866) was the youngest person on the expedition. The trip also shaped his later life.

Sacagawea's baby, Jean-Baptiste, or Pomp, was probably the best traveled baby in the United States! Riding on his mother's back, he had traveled nearly 5,000 miles (8,000 km) before he was two years old. On the expedition, William Clark became fond of Pomp. He asked Toussaint Charbonneau if he could raise the boy and pay for his education.

LEAVING HOME

After the expedition, Sacagawea and her family spent some time with Clark in St. Louis. In 1811, they went back to the Mandan village and left Pomp, then six years old, with Clark.

Pomp appears with his mother on the Sacagawea bronze dollar, first minted in 2000.

In 1848, Jean-Baptiste was one of the first men to join the California Gold Rush.

Clark educated Jean-Baptiste at home and later sent him to school. At the age of 18, the young man went to Europe for nearly six years in the service of a German duke. Jean-Baptiste learned to speak five languages. In 1829, he returned to the United States and followed in his father's footsteps as a fur trapper. In 1846, he guided soldiers to southern California during the Mexican-American War. After the war, he served briefly as a local mayor in California before joining the Gold Rush in 1848. He was a successful gold miner. When he decided to move to Montana in 1866, he died from pneumonia after falling into a river he was crossing.

William Clark paid for Pomp's education.

Back from THE PACIFIC

Sacagawea stayed with the Corps of Discovery to the end of its journey. Soon after, however, she faded from the historical record.

Sacagawea decided that she would remain with the Corps of Discovery. She left behind her Shoshone family and set out on the next part of the journey. She helped the Corps make the difficult journey over the Rockies through the Bitterroot Mountains. By the time they reached the other side of the mountains on September 23, 1805, they were nearly starving. The Nez Perce gave them food, before the expedition traveled via the Clearwater, Snake, and Columbia rivers to the Pacific Ocean. It was the middle of November 1805.

QUICK FACTS

- Sacagawea decided to leave her Shoshone family to continue with the expedition.
- She traveled almost 2,500 miles (4,000 km) from Fort Mandan to the Pacific Ocean!

Bozeman Pass became a major route for settlers heading west.

SETTLING DOWN

Lewis and Clark had successfully charted a route across North America from east to west, even if it was not **navigable**, as they had hoped.

Until the snow melted on the Rocky Mountains, it was too dangerous to attempt the return journey. That meant staying put for the winter. Sacagawea was allowed to vote with the rest of the Corps to decide the best place to build their winter camp. They voted to move from the north bank of the Columbia River to the south bank, where they had seen elk they might be able to hunt. There also seemed to be more shelter from harsh weather.

A LONG WINTER

On December 10, 1805, the men started to build a fort for the winter. They named it Fort Clatsop, for a friendly local Native American tribe. Sacagawea passed her time in the fort working. She cooked, dressed hides, made moccasins and clothes, and looked after Pomp. The weather was bad: it rained constantly. The men got sick because they had so little food, and what they did have never changed: elk meat and a few roots. The Europeans even ate dogs, but Sacagawea refused. They were running out of goods to barter with the Clatsop. At least they were warm in their wooden huts.

A reconstruction of Fort Clatsop.

CHRISTMAS

Sacagawea hunted white ermine for their tails.

When Christmas Day came, Sacagawea asked Charbonneau to explain what the holiday was about. He told her that people exchanged gifts on Christmas Day. Sacagawea decided to give Clark a present, because he was always so kind to her and Pomp (Clark called her Janey because he could not pronounce Sac-a-ga-wea). On Christmas Day, Lewis and Clark gave Sacagawea some beads and they gave Pomp toys they had made. She handed over her gift of 24 white ermine tails. Native Americans prized the tails, so it was a very special gift.

THE WHALE

Early in January, Sacagawea heard men talking about a dead whale that had washed up on the beach. She did not know what a whale was but she wanted to find out. Sacagawea herself had also still not seen the Pacific. Fort Clatsop was on the **estuary** of the Columbia River, rather than on the ocean itself.

Sacagawea asked Lewis and Clark if she could go to see the whale. It was the first time she had asked for a favor on the expedition. She and William Clark walked to the seashore, where she saw the body of the whale. Sacagawea was amazed by both the ocean and the whale.

THE JOURNEY BACK TO FORT MANDAN

On March 23, 1806, the Corps of Discovery started the long journey back east. They passed through Shoshone lands but, this time, Sacagawea did not meet anyone she knew. She decided to remain with her companions all the way back to Fort Mandan. When they were almost back, Pomp fell dangerously sick. For a week, Clark recorded in his diary, everyone was worried that the boy would not recover. To everyone's relief, by the beginning of June 1806 he was better.

Sacagawea said she had a right to go to see the whale as she had traveled so far with the expedition.

William Clark drew a map of the expedition's route.

SAYING GOODBYE

Back at Fort Mandan in August 1806, Charbonneau told Lewis and Clark he wanted to resume his life as a fur trader. Sacagawea, as his wife, had to stay with her husband. Charbonneau and Sacagawea said goodbye to the men of the Corps. Before he left, however, Clark promised that when Pomp was older he would pay for his education in St. Louis. Lewis and Clark returned to St. Louis and then went on to Washington, D.C. Their reports of their journey began a new age of westward expansion in North America.

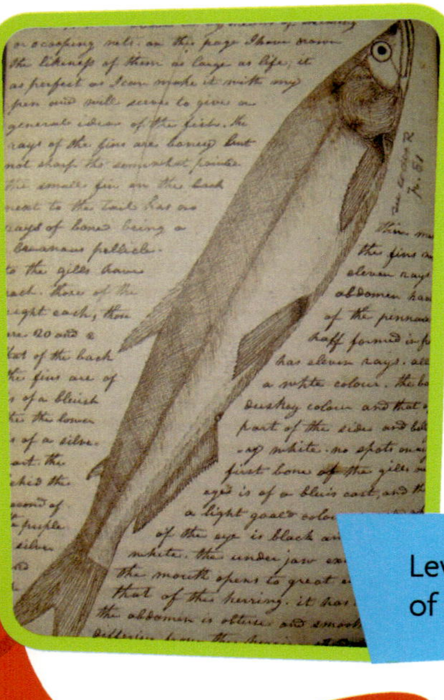

Lewis and Clark made notes and sketches of animals and plants they discovered.

WHAT HAPPENED NEXT?

No one really knows what happened to Sacagawea after the expedition. In some accounts, she had a daughter with Charbonneau. In April 1811, Charbonneau went to work for Manuel Lisa, a fur trader in Missouri. Sacagawea and their baby daughter Lisette went with him. It is thought that Sacagawea died from fever on a trading expedition on December 20, 1812. She was just 25 years old. However, a Shoshone story suggests that she lived longer and only died in 1885.

Sacagawea appeared on a US postal stamp in 1994.

Sacagawea's name largely vanished from history. It was revived in the early 20th century. Today, the contribution she made to opening up the West is widely recognized.

This statue of Sacagawea was created in 1905, when American **feminist** leaders became interested in her achievements.

Timeline

c. 1787
- Sacagawea is born, possibly near present-day Tendoy, Idaho.

1800
- Sacagawea is kidnapped by the Hidatsa during a hunt near Three Forks.

c. 1802
- Sacagawea becomes the second wife of fur trapper Toussaint Charbonneau.

1803
- April 30: The United States buys the Louisiana territory from France.

1804
- May 14: The Lewis and Clark expedition sets off up the Missouri River.
- October: The expedition arrives at the Hidatsa-Mandan village.
- November 4: Sacagawea meets Lewis and Clark.

1805
- February 11: Sacagawea gives birth to her son, Jean-Baptiste or Pomp.
- April 7: Sacagawea, Charbonneau, and Pomp set off with the Corps of Discovery.
- May 16: Sacagawea saves valuables when a canoe nearly capsizes.
- June 10: Sacagawea becomes seriously ill.
- August 8: Sacagawea recognizes her Shoshone homeland.
- November 15: The expedition reaches the Pacific Ocean.

1806
- January: Sacagawea sees the body of a dead whale.

- March 23: The Corps of Discovery leaves Fort Clatsop for the return journey.
- July: Lewis and Clark split up to explore different ways home. Sacagawea guides Clark over the Bozeman Pass.
- July 15: Clark's party reaches the Yellowstone River.
- August 12: The two parties reunite. The expedition reaches the Hidatsa-Mandan village.
- August 17: Sacagawea and Charbonneau quit the Corps of Discovery.

1811

- Sacagawea and her family travel to St. Louis to leave Pomp with William Clark.
- April 2: Sacagawea travels up the Missouri River with Charbonneau, who is now working for the Missouri Fur Company.

1812

- December 20: Around this time, Sacagawea possibly dies at Fort Manuel, in present-day South Dakota.

KEY DATES

- c. 1787 Sacagawea is born
- 1800 Kidnapped by the Hidatsa
- 1802 Marries Toussaint Charbonneau
- 1805 Gives birth to Jean-Baptiste. Joins the Corps of Discovery. Travels to the Pacific Ocean.
- 1806 Returns to the Hidatsa-Mandan village
- 1811 Leaves Jean-Baptiste with William Clark
- 1812 Possibly dies of fever in South Dakota

Glossary

capsizes Events when boats overturn.

colony A region or country ruled by another country.

commodity A raw material that is bought and sold.

constellations Groups of stars that form recognizable patterns.

Continental Divide A line across a continent on one side of which rivers drain in one direction and on the other side in the opposite direction.

estuary The mouth of a river where it meets the sea.

fauna The animals of a region.

feminist Someone who believes women should be treated equally to men.

flora The plants of a region.

fur trapper Someone who traps animals for their fur.

headwaters The small streams that form a river near its source.

hunter-gatherers People who live by hunting animals and gathering plants, nuts, and berries rather than by farming.

interpreters People who translate what someone says into another language.

lodges Small shelters built from wood or mud.

moccasins Soft leather shoes or slippers.

navigable Describes a river that can be traveled by boat.

navigation The act of finding one's way by following a route.

oriented Aligned or positioned in a particular direction.

papoose A baglike carrier that holds a child on an adult's back.

pelt The skin and fur of a dead animal.

romantic Idealized.

scale The size of something relative to something else.

spawn To release eggs.

staple Describes something basic.

status symbol Something that indicates someone's wealth or high social position.

tepees Conical tents made by stretching buffalo hides over poles.

wilderness An uninhabited, unwelcoming region.

Further Resources

Books

Crosby, Michael. *Sacagawea: Lewis and Clark's Pathfinder.* Stockton, NJ: OTTN Publishing, 2007.

Fradin, Dennis. *Who Was Sacagawea?* Who Was? New York: Grosset and Dunlap, 2002.

Gunderson, Jessica, and Cynthia Martin. *Sacagawea: Journey into the West.* Graphic Biographies. Mankato, Minn: Capstone Press, 2006.

Morley, Jacqueline. *You Wouldn't Want to Explore with Lewis and Clark.* You Wouldn't Want to... New York: Franklin Watts, 2013.

Petrie, Kristin. *Sacagawea.* Explorers. Edina, Minn.: Abdo Publishing Company, 2007.

Sutcliffe, Jane. *Sacagawea.* History Maker Bios. Minneapolis: Lerner Publications, 2009.

Websites

Biography.com
www.biography.com/people/sacagawea-9468731
A detailed biography of Sacagawea from Biography.com.

Ducksters
www.ducksters.com/biography/explorers/sacagawea.php
Ducksters.com has a biography of Sacagawea.

National Geographic
www.nationalgeographic.com/west/
An interactive challenge based on Lewis and Clark's journey.

United States Mint
www.usmint.gov/kids/games/lewisclarkadventure/
The U.S. Mint has a fun game based on the Corps of Discovery.

Publisher's note to educators and parents: Our editors have carefully reviewed these websites to ensure that they are suitable for students. Many websites change frequently, however, and we cannot guarantee that a site's future contents will continue to meet our high standards of quality and educational value. Be advised that students should be closely supervised whenever they access the Internet.

Index

A
artichokes 29
Asia 26

B
beaver 24
Bismarck, North Dakota 18
Bitterroot Mountains 11, 13, 36
Bozeman Pass 38
buffalo 9, 11, 12, 19

C
Cameahwait 33
canoes 29, 31
capture, Sacagawea 16
Charbonneau, Jean-Baptiste 23, 26, 28, 32, 34, 35, 40, 41, 42
Charbonneau, Lisette 43
Charbonneau, Pomp, *see* Charbonneau, Jean-Baptiste
Charbonneau, Toussaint 19, 20, 22, 23, 25, 31, 40, 42, 43
Christmas 40
Clark, William 4, 21, 22, 23, 28, 32, 33, 34, 35, 40, 41, 42
Clatsop 39
Columbia River 36, 38, 40
constellations 15
Continental Divide 8
Corps of Discovery 22, 26, 29, 30, 36, 31

D E
death, Sacagawea 43
elk 38

F
farming 18
food 9, 12, 29
Fort Clatsop 39, 40
Fort Mandan 22, 26, 41, 42
fur trappers 19, 20, 24, 25
furs 19, 24

G H I J
Gold Rush 35
Hidatsa 9, 16, 18, 19, 20
horses 11, 23, 33
Idaho 6, 8, 10
Jefferson, Thomas 4

L
landscape 13
Lemhi River 10
Lemhi Shoshone *see* Shoshone
Lewis, Meriwether 4, 21, 22, 23, 33, 40, 42
Lisa, Manuel 43
lodges 18, 19
Louisiana 4

M
Mandan 18
maps 14, 15
marriage, Sacagawea 13, 20
Mexican-American War 35
Missouri River 4, 11, 22, 26, 31
Montana 8

N
name, Sacagawea 8, 9
navigation 14, 15
New France 24
Nez Perce 36
Northern Shoshone *see* Shoshone

P R
Pacific Ocean 4, 26, 36
Rocky Mountains 8, 33, 36, 38

S
salmon 10
Salmon River 8, 10
Seaman, dog 26
Shoshone 6, 10, 11, 12, 13, 33, 41
St. Louis 34, 42

T
tepees 12
Three Forks 11
transportation 11, 29, 31

U W
United States 6
Utah 10
Washington, D.C. 42
Washington, George 6
weather 13
whale 40, 41